D0230835

What lies within the
Shopping Days
Fabric Project Book

Concentration Level

○ Nice and relaxing... let's day dream

○○ This is fun

○○○ Mmmm, let's think

○○○○ Put the coffee on, white no sugar

Florrie

Shopping List

Large button hook

2oz of claggy toffee

Fork handles

Tin of elbow grease

Fabric for a rag doll

Comic book for Norman

Pay insurance at the Co-op

1 yard of pretty fabric (avoid the serge)

Colliery Days Fabric Project book

Betty

Daily Errands

Box of beeswax candles

Collect 4 candles

Tin of dubbin for father's boots

6 assorted postcards

2 yds of knicker elastic

Deposit 2 shillings into bank account

Sheet music (Harry Fragson, 'Hello, hello who's your lady friend')

Getting Ready

The Smartest Dolls in Town

*They are known as the
    smartest dolls in town
Their names are
    Betty and Florrie
Miss Florrie has pretty blue eyes
Miss Betty's are brown and jolly
They go to town and
    strut their stuff
And when they think they
    have had enough
It's off to the smartest place
    for tea
The pert Miss Florrie and
    the saucy Miss B!*

Betty

NORTH EASTERN RAILWAY.
HISTORIC YORK
THE THRESHOLD OF
ENGLAND'S BEST
HOLIDAY GROUND

Betty's Big Bag

Weekend trips to Newcastle

florrie

The inspiration for this bag came from the large carpet bags carried in the Edwardian Period. Handbags were not popular at the time. Large bags were carried for travelling and small evening bags were used by the more affluent women. Our bag is ideal for overnight stays and shopping.

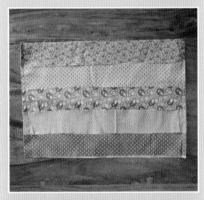

What you need

Duck Cloth 50cms (½ Yard)	15 x 2½" strips (1 m fabric in total)
Border fabric 15cms (5")	Lining fabric 50cms (½ Yard)
Handles 20cms (8")	
Wadding 60cms (24")	4 x grommets

Finished Size: 19" x 20" approx

Cutting

If not using Jelly Roll Strips
Cut 15 x 2½" strips WOF, and cut in half

Duck Cloth cut 2 x 20" x 17"

Border cut 2 x 4½" x 19½"

Handles cut 4 x" x 21" strips

Wadding cut 2 x 19" x 21½", 2 x 1½" strips

Lining cut 2 x 19½" x 20½"

How to make it

Place the Duck Cloth on a flat surface with the long edge on the horizontal.

Place 7 of the 2½" strips across the horizontal of the Duck cloth, so that the long sides butt up with each other. Pin in place and sew each of the short sides approx ⅛" from the sides. This keeps them in place. **See photo.**

Take another 2½" strip and starting at the left hand side weave the strip under the first horizontal fabric and over the second, continue until you reach the top. Pin in place. Weave the second strip in a similar manner but start by weaving over the first horizontal fabric and under the second fabric. Pin in place. **See photo.**

Repeat until the whole piece is covered.

Sew the border fabric to the shorter edge of the bag. Press.

Place on top of the wadding and sew each of the woven strips in place through the wadding. We used a decorative stitch on the machine.

CAUGHT IN THE ACT

An opportune thief was caught in the act yesterday. As Miss Betty posed for photographs for a quilting editorial, the culprit, as yet unidentified, struck.

She was captured on film by the press who were covering the event. She even laughed as they photographed her!

A ten shilling note was found to be missing from the till.

Sgt Biff is the officer in charge of the case. He believes she is from the toon, because she has 'that sort of look about her'.

Anyone having any information about the incident should contact Beamish Police on Beamish 767. She will be shown the error of her ways, the ten bob will be recovered and there will be no arrests.

FANCY KNICKE KNOCKE

Ladies are being advised to check washing lines or days after a spe of thefts of ladie undergarments. police spokesma Sgt Biff advised that these thefts occurred in the end of the town. He stated "from eyewitness repo suspect is a you who makes off down the back l From past exper the suspects col these garments; however, due to fancy lace work on the items, ma victims are reluc identify any gar which have been recovered!"

He warns young l to come forward and assist him in enquiries.

There have been arrests.

6D-

The Templeton Twins

The Templeton twins are
*   dressmakers*
The finest in the town
If you need something
*   rather special*
Like a bag or a stunning
*   ball gown*
Their designs are
*   really beautiful*
They are truly talented
*   and kind*
So don't delay,
*   pay a visit today*
It's amazing what you'll find

Betty

Betty's Big Bag

Trim the finished piece to 19½" x 20½". Repeat to make the other side of the bag.

Place the two outside pieces RST and sew down the sides and along the bottom of the bag.

Make a paper bag bottom. See Work Basket.

To make the lining place the fabrics RST and sew the 2 long sides and a short side, leaving a gap in one of the long sides, for turning through. Make a paper bag bottom as before.

Place the bag lining inside the bag RST. Matching seams, pin around the top edge and sew in place.

Turn the bag through the lining, and press. Top stitch around the top of the bag.

To make the handles, place the fabric RST and put on top of the wadding. Sew down the long sides and turn through. You can shorten the handles at this stage if required. Neaten the ends.

To insert the grommets, measure 5" in from the side edge of the border and half an inch from the woven panel. Mark the inside circle of the grommet. Cut the centre circle out taking care that the outside and lining of the bag are matched. Insert the grommet as per the manufacturer's instructions. Repeat for the other side. Refer to Photo for placement.

To attach the handles thread them through the grommets and sew them in place.

Betty's Tip

This bag looks as though it is pieced.

The weaving technique gives the same result without having to match the seams.

The construction of the bag is therefore quick and easy.

Florrie's Hooky Bag

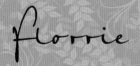
Every house has several Hooky or Proggy mats so we incorporated the hooky technique into this bag. (See Colliery Days for the proggy technique). The hooky band around this bag adds texture. This delightful little bag is ideal for carrying those little essentials or makes a really special gift bag.

What you need

Fabric A:
Outside bag 15cms (6")

Fabric B:
Lining Fat 8th

Hessian
5cms x 30cms (2" x 11")

Wadding 15cms (6")

2 Buttons

Crotchet hook

Scraps of fabric

Finished Size: 16" x 4½" approx (including handle)

Cutting

Fabric A cut 1 x 5½" x 5", cut 2 x 5½" squares and cut handle 1 x 20" x 2"

Fabric B cut 5½" x 18"

Hessian 2 x 5½" x 2"

Scraps cut into ½" strips

Wadding cut 1 x 5½" x 20"

How to make it

Please note In this project we have used ½" seams for the main construction of the outer bag.

See photo and sew the fabrics and hessian together, with the 5½" x 5" piece in the middle.

Start at the bottom right hand side (if you are right handed) of each piece of hessian as shown in photo. Lay the strip of fabric under the hessian and using a crotchet hook, start ½" in from the edge and push the hook down into the hessian and pull up a loop of fabric. Repeat along the row, keeping the loops a similar size. **See photo.** Complete one row at a time and then work in the same direction for the remaining rows until the hessian is covered.

Layer the outer bag onto the wadding and quilt as desired. Trim wadding.

Fold into a tube RST, matching seams, and sew sides. Turn through.

To make the handles fold fabric in half RST lengthwise, sew the long edge turn through and press.

Position the handles onto the outer bag, baste in place.

To make the lining, fold RST and sew sides. Insert lining into bag, turning over the top edge to form a binding, sew in the handles. **See photo.** Embellish with buttons.

An example of the proggy technique can be found in Colliery Days.

A FORM OF ARTISTIC EXPRESSION

Hand made mats were a great way for people to be creative. Examples of elaborate designs and colours are on show at Beamish Museum. Regional styles and patterns became evident with unique designs coming from different places.

Mats were ideal for houses where the men came in with their boots on, taking your shoes off was not standard practice, and houses were cold so shoes or clogs were worn all the time. Hooky and Proggy mats had to be easy to move and take ootside for a good shake.

TRIANGLE CONUNDR...

The local Quilt... society was lef... perplexed after... by a well know... who visited the...

Her talk on qui... construction lef... members needi... sustenance and... ache relief!

Her triangles ca... many problems... they the right si... they the correct... The list was en...

As one member... commented 'she... doesn't seem to... her Isosceles fr... Equilateral!

Next month she... with the Drunka... Path, confused?... will be!

9

Folded Brooch & Button Rings

Brooches were the finishing touch to an outfit in 1913. We have used a paper folding technique with fabric to create these unusual brooches. They are also ideal for adding interest to boxes, bags, cushions, wall hangings etc.

The rings have endless possibilities with colours and sizes and they are very easy to make. We saw some beautiful buttons in the Co-op at Beamish Museum, on cards in the haberdashery department and on the period costumes exhibited.

Offer a Kiss

Her name is simply Betty
She's a quirky little Miss
The boys creep up behind her
And they try to steal a kiss
She speaks to them
*   quite sternly*
And she says this isn't proper
When I am ready to be kissed
Then I will make the offer

What you need

Florrie's Folded Brooches	Betty's Button Rings
Squares of fabric 10cms (8 x 3" squares)	Strips of felt 2cms x 8cms (¾" x 3")
Heat 'n' Bond Ultra	Assorted buttons
Button	Threads
Scrap of felt	Strong glue

Florrie's Folded Brooches

Finished Size: 4" x 4" approx

How to make it

Fuse the Heat 'n' Bond Ultra to the reverse of the fabric squares. See Work Basket. Remove the backing paper of the Heat 'n' Bond Ultra.

Take one square and fold WST on both the diagonals to crease. **See step by step photo.** Now fold the square in half RST in both directions. **See photo.** Refer to photo for final fold to form a triangle.

Press each triangle using an iron, the Heat 'n' Bond will fuse together. Make 8 in total, trimming the long edges to neaten.

Place the triangles together to form the medallion, gluing each one in place as you go.

See photo for the placement. Please note the last triangle has to be fitted into the first triangle. Allow to dry.

Cut a square of felt slightly smaller than your finished brooch, glue into place on the reverse. Embellish with a button. Add a brooch back or safety pin to finish.

Betty's Button Rings

Finished Size: 1" x 1" approx

How to make it

Fold the felt strips in half lengthwise and sew along each edge. Cut the felt to fit your finger, and stitch the short edges together to form a ring.

Layer your buttons on top of each other to create your own design (**See photo** for inspiration) and glue or sew them onto the felt ring, covering the join.

A combination of glueing & sewing makes a stronger finished ring.

Time Pieced Station Clock

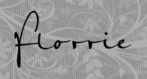

The railway station is full of the nostalgia and romance of steam engines and of course the trains ran on time, they ran like clockwork.

Beamish Museum has some unique clocks. We have taken the idea of a patchwork time piece and designed this quirky clock. Patchwork that tells you the time – fab.

What you need

Fabric A 25cms (9")

Fabric B 25cms (9")

Fabric C Fat 16th

Fabric D backing fabric Fat Quarter

Wadding Fat Quarter

Fabric E binding 15cms (6")

Heat 'n' Bond Lite

4 buttons

Clock mechanism

Finished Size: 16" x 16" approx

Cutting

Fabric A cut 10 x 4½" squares

Fabric B cut 10 x 4½" squares

Fabric D cut 16" x 16"

Fabric E cut 2 x 2½" strips

Heat 'n' Bond Lite make one circle (template F) from page 55

How to make it

Take 2 Fabric A squares and fold in half on the diagonal WST and press. Repeat for Fabric B.

Place the folded A fabrics on top of 2 Fabric B squares, and place the folded B Fabrics onto 2 Fabric A squares. Baste in place on the outer edges. These are the corner squares. **See photo.**

Refer to the photo for placement and sew 4 rows of 4 squares.

Fuse the circle of Heat 'n' Bond Lite to Fabric C, and then fuse this circle to the centre of the pieced square.

Stitch in place, we used a blanket stitch.

On each of the corner squares, roll back the folded fabric and stitch in place. This gives a curve to the square. **See photo.**

Layer with wadding and backing fabric, quilt as desired.

After trimming the edges bind using your preferred method or see Work Basket.

Baste

Baste

Add buttons where the numbers are on the clock face.

Make a Button hole in the centre of the clock face using your preferred method or see Work Basket.

Fit the clock Mechanism, available from your local craft store.

The Co-op Store

If you wanted a tin bath or washboard the Co-op was the place to go

Aye the Co-op was the place to go. Everywhere had one, our local one opened in 1910. Mam had her own 'divi' number and you collected a share at intervals during the year. It sold everything you would need from food to tin baths and washboards. The food was not pre-packed like it is now; you could get butter by the ounce and bacon sliced to your liking. We would gan to the Co-op haberdashery when we'd saved enough to get the material for to make things. I loved it in there.

florrie

Florrie's Medallion Quilt

Simply Betty

I made a large quilt when I was young to cover the settee in front of the fire. It started off as tapestry but with the coal fire things got really dirty, it got greasy looking and I hated owt that looked grubby so I decided to make a quilt, I bought the material with my sewing money, it was pretty expensive but nowt like it is now. It was maroon and yellow, different floral patterns, it was canny. Mam wanted me to use old stuff we had in the house but I wanted a new one, I'm not sure she was ever very happy about it, she was always careful was mam.

Beamish Museum has a fantastic collection of old quilts. We have studied the different designs and taken elements from a few to create our own homage to the period. The Sanderson Star appears in several of the quilts. We have taken a simpler star shape as inspiration for the centre of our quilt. By making a Medallion quilt you can make a quilt to any size you wish.

What you need

Centre square
Fabric 1 x 5" square
Fabric 2 10cms (4")
Fabric 3 (red) Fat Quarter
Fabric 4 Fat 8th

Flying Geese
40cms (16")
of a minimum of 2 fabrics

Square in a square blocks
Fabric 1 (centre) 30cms (12")
Fabric 2 40cms (14")
Fabric 3 70cms (28")

Triangle border
total of 2m (78")

Border fabric
(blue on quilt) 1.2m (46")

Corner stone fabric
40cms (16")

Binding 60cms (20")

Backing fabric
108" wide 2m (78")

Wadding
90" wide 2m (78")

Finished Size: 73" x 73" approx

How to make it

Centre square

Finished Size 18" square

The centre is made up of 3 blocks which are then sewn together.

To make the centre square in this block cut 1 x 4¾" square and 2 x 3⅞" squares from a different fabric. Cut the 3⅞" squares in half on the diagonal to yield 4 triangles.

Sew a triangle to 2 opposite sides, press and repeat for the remaining 2.

To make the corner squares, using 2 different fabrics cut 2 x 6⅞" squares from each.

Place one square of each colour RST, draw a diagonal line across the square and sew a ¼" either side of the drawn line. Cut on the line and press. Make 4 in total.

To make the triangle blocks make template A and B on page 54. Cut out 4 of template A, 4 of template B and 4 of template B reversed. Sew a template B and a template B reversed to each side of the template A triangles. Make 4, **see photo 1.**

Referring to the main photo of the quilt sew the blocks together to complete the centre square.

Trim to 18½".

First Border

Cut 2 x 3½" x 18½" and 2 x 3½" x 24½" strips from the Border fabric.

Sew the 18½" strips to the sides of the quilt, press and add the remaining two strips to the other sides. The quilt will now measure 24½".

Flying Geese Border

Finished size of each block 6" x 3"

You need to make a total of 32 flying geese. This technique yields 4 flying geese blocks from 2 squares of fabric. To make 4 geese, cut 1 x 7½" square for the geese and 1 x 8½" square for the sky.

Take a geese square and a sky square and centre the geese on the top of the sky square RST. There will be a ½" seam allowance all around. Draw a diagonal line and sew both sides of the line using a ¼" seam allowance. **See photo 2.**

Cut on the drawn line and press towards the dark fabric.

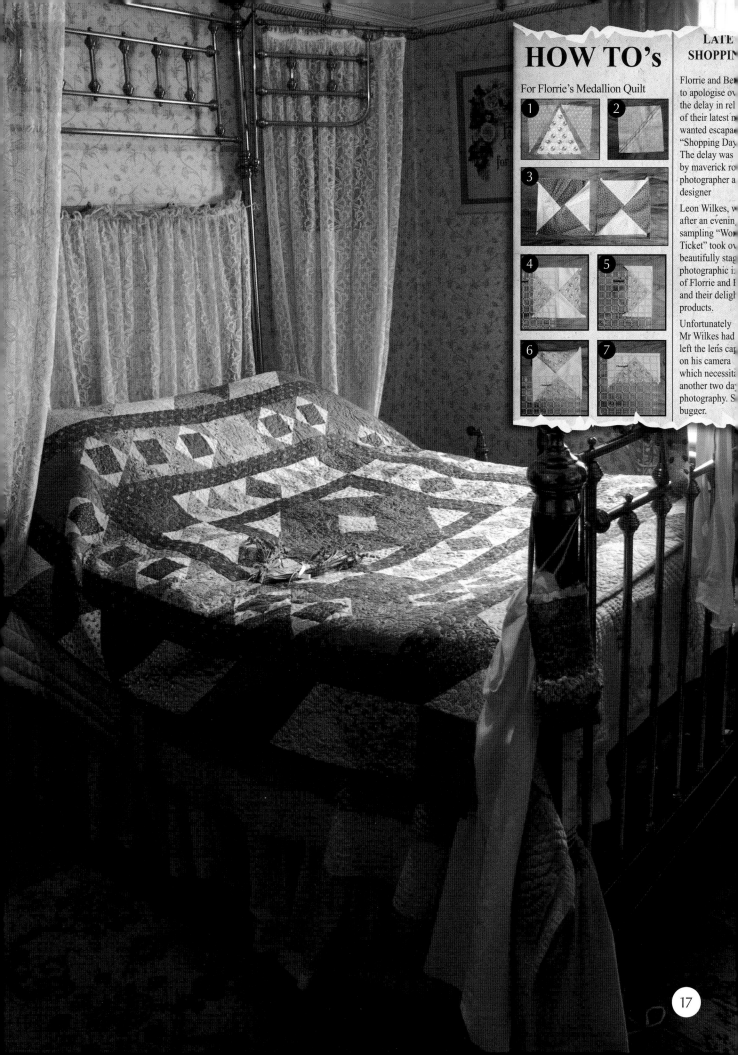

HOW TO's

For Florrie's Medallion Quilt

1 2 3 4 5 6 7

LATE
SHOPPIN

Florrie and Be
to apologise ov
the delay in rel
of their latest
wanted escape
"Shopping Day
The delay was
by maverick ro
photographer a
designer

Leon Wilkes, w
after an evenin
sampling "Wo
Ticket" took ov
beautifully stag
photographic i
of Florrie and
and their deligh
products.

Unfortunately
Mr Wilkes had
left the lens cap
on his camera
which necessita
another two day
photography. S
bugger.

Florrie's Medallion Quilt

A New Corset

Florrie needs a new corset

Betty a pretty new vest

They like to visit the Co-op

For they have the very best

Of lovely scarves and hats

Print fabrics cut ready to go

With their shopping done

They've had so much fun

It's time to head

home and sew.

Betty

Position these 2 squares RST matching the corners with no seams. Ensure the sky is on the top of the geese fabric. There will be excess fabric on the corners with the seams don't worry about this. Draw a diagonal line on the corners with no seams and sew a ¼" either side of the line. Cut on the drawn line and press.

Trim the geese to 6½" x 3½", it is easier use a bias square ruler. To do this look at the 2 sections you have just made and you will see that one of the pieces will have a vertical geese and the other will have a horizontal geese, **see photo 3**.

Trim the section with the vertical geese, first align the top point of the geese with the point where the 3¼" line (this is one half of the unfinished width of the geese), meets the bias square's diagonal line, aligning the 6½" line where the 2 fabrics intersect, trim along both edges of the ruler, **see photo 4**. Flip the segment and trim the other sides.

Now trim the left hand side geese by moving the bias square so that the 3½" line is along the bottom of the geese and the 3 ¼" mark is through the top of the geese, **see photo 5**. Cut along the sides of the bias square. It will now measure 6½" x 3½". Turn and trim the remaining segment in the same way.

To trim the horizontal geese align the top point of the upper geese triangle where the point meets 3¼" on the bias rulers diagonal line, aligning the 6½" line at the point where the 2 fabrics intersect, trim along the ruler edges, **see photo 6**. Turn and trim the remaining sides.

Move the square to the lower geese and position the 3½" line along the bottom edge and the 3¼" line through the top point of the geese triangle, **see photo 7**. Cut along the sides of the ruler. Repeat for the other geese.

Make a total of 32 flying geese. Refer to photo for placement and join 8 flying geese together. Repeat 3 more times.

Sew a row to opposite sides.

Cut 4 x 6½" squares from the corner stone fabric. Add a square to each end of the remaining strips. Sew these to the top and bottom of the quilt.

The quilt now should measure 36½" square.

Third Border

Cut 2 x 3½" x 36½" and 2 x 3½" x 42½" strips from the Border fabric, sew these to the quilt in the same manner as Border 1.

The quilt will now measure 42½".

Square in a Square border

Finished size of block 7"

For each block you need at least 3 different fabrics. Cut 24 x 4" squares from one fabric, cut 48 x 3½" squares from another and cut these in half on the diagonal, and from a third fabric cut 48 x 4½" squares, and cut these in half on the diagonal.

Sew 2 of the small triangles to the opposite sides of a 4" square, press and sew another 2 of these triangles to the remaining sides, press. Check that the block measures 5½" square, trim if necessary.

Sew 2 of the larger triangles to the opposite sides of the block as before, press and sew two more to the remaining sides, press. Check that the block measures 7½" square, trim if necessary.

Refer to the photo and sew the blocks into 4 rows of 6. Sew of 2 these rows to the sides of the quilt, press.

Cut 4 x 7½" squares from the corner stone fabric. Add one of these to each end of the remaining strips and sew onto the quilt as before.

The quilt should now measure 56½" square.

Fifth Border

Cut 2 x 3½" x 56½" strips and 2 x 3½" x 62½" strips.

Sew these to the quilt in the same manner as Border 1.

Triangle Border

Cut a total of 48 templates C, from assorted fabrics and 2 x template D, and 2 x template D reversed see page 54.

Sew 12 template C triangles together, to make a long strip. Add a template D to each end of the 4 strips. **See photo** for placement.

Sew 2 of these strips to sides.

Cut 4 x 6" square from the corner stone fabric. Add one of these to each end of the remaining strips and sew onto the quilt as before.

The quilt should now measure 73" x 73".

Layer up quilt and quilt as desired.

Bind the quilt using your preferred method see Work Basket.

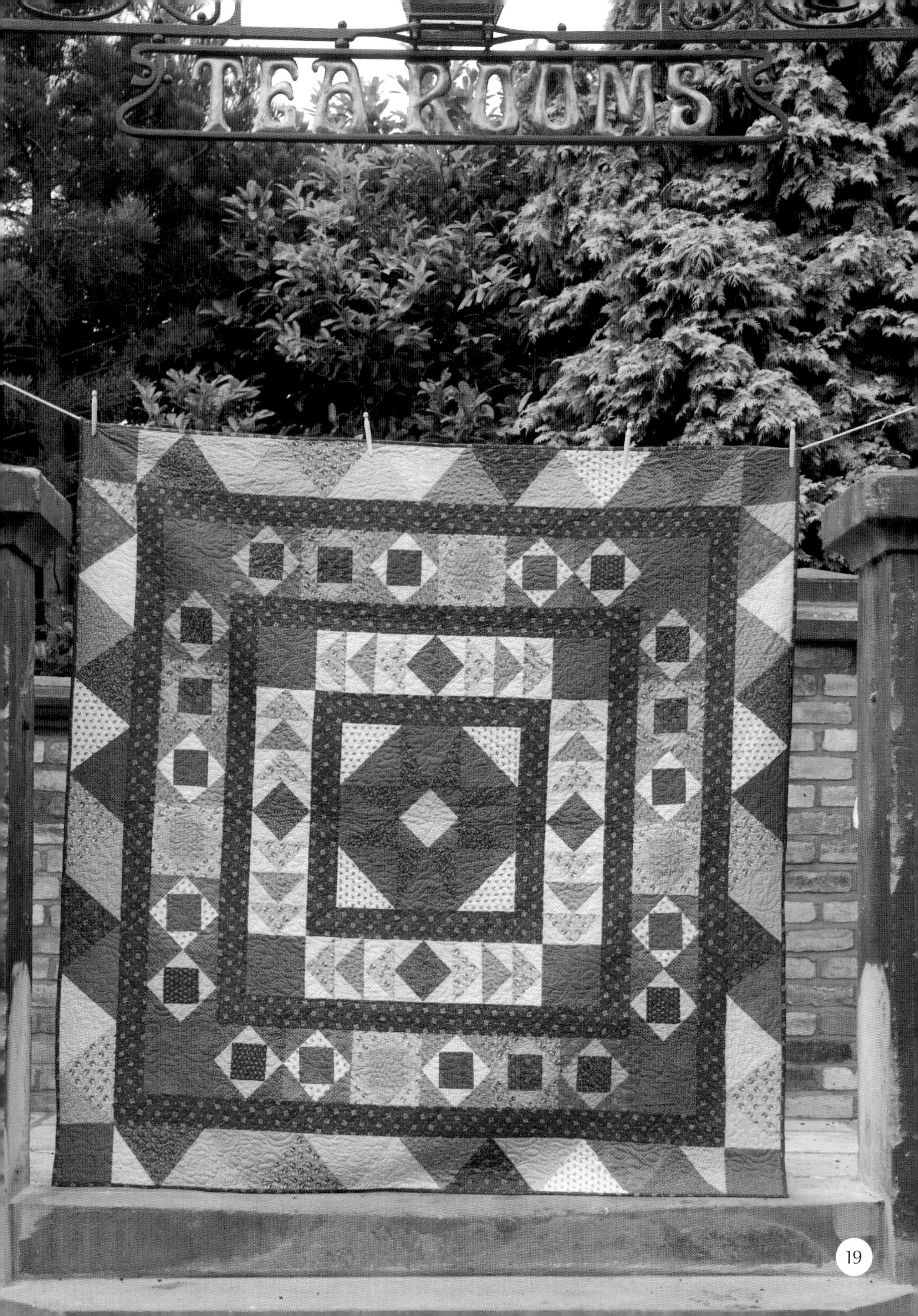
TEA ROOMS

Tree of Co-operation

Crème de la Peppermints (Betty's posh mints)

You will need

8oz (225g) icing sugar

Half teaspoon peppermint extract

6 tablespoons condensed milk

Pop the sugar in a bowl and add the condensed milk and extract a bit at a time to form a dough or 'fadge' as Betty likes to call it.

Knead the fadge and then roll it out to a minty depth (approx ¼")

Use a shaped cutter to make the mints and lay these on baking paper to dry.

You should be able to make over 20 mints with this mixture – remember to share!

Betty

On the wall of the Insurance office in the Co-operative store, is a large picture of a tree depicting the Women's Co-operative Guild. We have taken this as inspiration for our tree, adding those people who are special in ours lives. Try making detachable apples for a rewards tree for children.

What you need

Background fabric 60cms (23")	Optional printable fabric for photos
Fabric for tree 30 cms (12")	Wadding 60cms (23")
Assorted fabrics for leaves and apples	Backing fabric 60 cms (23")
Binding 25cms (10")	Heat 'n' Bond Lite
Embroidery threads	

Finished Size: 21" x 32" approx

Cutting

Background fabric cut 22" x 35"

Wadding cut 22" x 35"

Binding cut 4 x 2½" strips

How to make it

Trace the tree (templates L, M & N), leaves (templates P & O) & apples (template R) onto Heat 'n' Bond Lite using the templates on Pages 56-57.

Refering to the photo for placement, fuse the pieces to the background fabric. If you wish to add photos (follow the manufacturers instructions) fuse them to the background fabric at this stage.

Stitch around each appliquéd piece, Betty used a blanket stitch. You can also add buttons or embellishments of your choice.

Layer up the wall hanging (see Work Basket) and quilt as desired. Trim the background to 21"x 32" and bind using your preferred method or see the Work Basket.

To hang the Tree of Co-operation add a hanging sleeve, or tabs. See Work Basket.

The tree could also be framed.

AGENT FOR THE
CO-OPERATIVE INSURANCE
SOCIETY L^{TD}
JOINT INSURANCE DEP^T
OF THE C.W.S. & S.C.W.S.

Chocolate Stitchery

Divine Chocolate Cake

Miss Millicent Maude is a

wonderful cook

The best for miles around

Her pies are sweet and

succulent

The best that can be found

They say her cakes are light

as love

The trifles quite sublime

With scones so truly

scrumptious

And chocolate cake divine

Betty

The Sweet Shop is located next to the printers and is filled with every thing children young and old could imagine. Hundreds of jars cover the shelves and old fashioned cinder toffee and sherbets are for sale. Inspired by the advertising signs for confectionary, our stitchery promotes Florrie and Betty's Chocolates. If only they were real.

What you need

Background fabric 30cms x 25cms (12" x 10")	Weaveline 30cms x 25cms (12" x 10")
Brown stranded embroidery thread	

Finished Size: 12" x 10" approx

How to make it

Trace the stitchery pattern on Page 59 onto the centre of the background fabric. Place the weaveline on the back.

All stitching is completed with 2 strands of embroidery thread.

We had our stitchery framed.

See the workbasket for the guide to the stitches we have used.

This stitchery looks lovely made into a simple wall hanging, cushion or used as a panel for a bag.

Florrie's Tip

When framing your stitchery try to choose frames and inserts that compliment the fabrics and colours.

For our chocolate stichery, we have chosen shades of brown to create a neutral look. Varying the shades slightly.

If we have stitched in bright colours we would have chosen complimentary colours for a totally different effect.

23

Bonny Boot Cushion

Glamorous Bag and Shoes

Sarah Anne is quite a fan

Of glamorous bags and shoes

When she's depressed

> *she's up and dressed*

And goes shopping

> *to help her blues*

She may buy a coat,

> *perhaps a hat*

She will spend on this,

> *and spend on that*

But the very last thing

> *that she will chose*

Is a glamorous bag

> *and glamorous shoes*

The clothing department in the Co-operative Store has examples of vintage clothing and accessories. Boots were the popular footwear of the period, fastened with buttons which were closed with the help of a button hook. Our scented cushions take inspiration from these shapes, by adding your own buttons, lace and trimmings you can make a unique piece.

What you need

Fabric 20cms (8")
per boot

A scrap of muslin to make
a small packet for lavender

Toy filling

Buttons

Trimmings

Finished Size: 8" x 6" approx

Cutting

Boot cut 1 x 17"x8"

Hanger cut 1 x 8" x 2"

Muslin cut 2 x 2" x 1"

How to make the Muslin Bag

Sew the two pieces together on three sides, fill with dried lavender or star anise, sew opening closed.

How to make the Boot

Make a freezer paper template AA on page 61.

Fold fabric in half RST.

Sew around the boot leaving the top open, cut out using pinking shears.

Turn through and stuff firmly, adding the lavender bag.

Fold hanger fabric in half along the long edge RST and sew.

Turn through and press, fold in half.

Insert the folded hanger into the top of the boot, turn under a small hem and whip stitch to close.

Add buttons and trimmings. **See photo.**

If you wish you can scent the boots with drops of essential oil added to the toy filling. They can be hung in wardrobes, on handles or added to drawers or shoe boxes.

Margaret Grace

Loved Buying Shoes

I used to make modesty vests out of satin and ribbon at home and sell them for 3d and I made cheval sets for a shilling. The money was then mine to spend. I handed over my pay from skivvying to Mam and got pocket money back. With that money I had to buy my shoes and things. My sewing money bought those extra bits and pieces, the frivolous things I couldn't have had otherwise. I remember I went to Ryals in Whitley Bay, it was a posh shop and used to have good stuff in there, I bought a lovely two piece with the money I'd saved sewing for the ladies in the village.

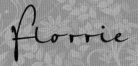

Margaret Grace is inspired by the advertising memorabilia in the Grocery Department in the Co-operative Store. Rag or cloth dolls were popular with children in the period, easy to make and lovely to cuddle.

What you need

Fabric for body Fat 8th	Lace (optional)
Fabric for dress 30cms (12")	8 small buttons
Fabric for ruffle Fat 8th	Straw hat & basket (available from Craft Shops), decorative buttons (optional)
Toy filling	
Freezer paper	

Finished Size: 13" tall, approx

Cutting

Ruffle cut 1 x 19" x 4"

How to make it

Fold the body fabric in half and make freezer paper templates of the body, legs & hands see templates BB, CC & DD on page 61. Using the templates as a guide sew, leaving openings as indicated on the pattern pieces. Cut out the pieces with pinking shears, turn through & stuff to where indicated on the pattern. Insert the legs into the bottom of the body and sew the opening closed.

To make the dress

Using the template EE on Page 61 cut out 2 pieces on the fold of the dress fabric. With RST sew around leaving openings as indicated on the pattern. Turn through and press. Neaten the neck, hemline and sleeve edges with a small hem.

Insert the arms into the sleeve openings, stitch in place & add buttons. **See photo.**

Embellish the dress. We added lace to the hemline, now fit the dress to the doll.

To make the neck ruffle fold the fabric in half lengthwise RST. Sew along the long edge, turn through and press. The ruffle is made by gathering the fabric around the dolls neck. Use a running stitch, sew along the long edge of the ruffle and gather to fit. Pull tightly to give definition to the neck. Secure in place with a small stitch.

Glue or stitch the hat on her. If adding a basket stitch the hands together so Margaret Grace can hold it.

We have filled the basket with fruit buttons.

Starch

eckitt's

per lb.

METAL
POLISH

Starch

ckitt's

CRU

SOAP

WITCH
SOAP

JEYE

LIFEB

LIFEBUOY

FOR SAVING LIFE
FOR PRESERVATION OF HEALTH

SOAP

SENALIA

LIFEBUOY

FOR SAVING LIFE
FOR PRESERVATION OF HEALTH

SOAP

Taking Care of Business

Little Betty Bloomers

Little Betty Bloomers
Has limited time to shop
She needs to deposit a cheque
And has parcels
*   she needs to drop*
Her bicycle needs repairing
A paper she needs to pick up
Perhaps then she'll
*   stop for refreshment*
Of tea in a bone china cup

Betty

28

Norman the Naughty...

The Naughty Newspaper Boy

Norman is a naughty one

A cheeky little man

He pushes Florrie off the tree

As often as he can

But Florrie's having none of this

She's made it very plain

If he does it one more time

He's outside in the rain

Beamish Museum has an interesting printing and stationary shop with an advert for delivery boys. We thought we could fill the vacancy and Norman was born. He is ready for work with his bag and newspapers but is always ready for a bit of mischief armed with his catapult! A knitting pattern for his cap and scarf is included.

What you need

Calico for body 40cms (16")	Fabric for shorts 40cms (16")
Fabric for shirt 30cms (12")	1" buckle
Felt 3 colours 30cm (12")	Assorted buttons
Toy filling	Freezer paper
Lolly stick	Pigma pen
Hair	

Finished Size: 25" tall approx

How to make it

To make the body

Fold calico in half and make freezer paper templates FF of body parts on Page 62-63. Using the templates as a guide sew the body pieces leaving openings for legs, arms and bottom of the body. Cut out the pieces with pinking sheers and turn through. Stuff the body, arms & legs as indicated on the pattern. When stuffing the body put the lolly stick in the neck, this will make sure it remains straight. Insert the legs into the bottom of the body and sew the opening closed. Sew the arms to the side of the body. Wrap the hair around the head and stitch in place. **See photo.**

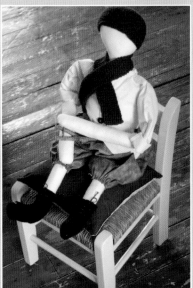

To make the shirt

Make paper freezer paper templates GG on Page 63. Hem all the edges now. Sew the front pieces to the back piece, RST. Turn through and press. Fit to Norman, adding 3 buttons to the shirt. If you think the shirt is too small at his stage don't worry when you sew the front pieces together and pull tightly it forms a V neck.

To make the shorts

Make a freezer paper template HH on page 63. Cut out 4. Put 2 of these pieces RST and sew along the curved edge.

WANTED

A Few Respectable Boys
to sell the

NORTHERN DAILY MAIL

8s. to 12s. per week easily
earned by pushing Boys

Apply 4
Mail Office

STOP PRESS

Naughty Norman the newspaper boy has been barred from the Co-operative Store in Beamish.

Whilst he was queuing for a pound of broken biscuits, he was heard singing loudly a song which made reference to a fly in the Co-op store that did something on the ceiling and something on the floor, something on the bacon and something on the ham, but before he could finish his rendition, he was ejected by the Co-op man.

Mrs Winstanley who runs the stationers was said to be shocked at such behaviour from her number one delivery boy.

EXHIBIT ONION TWIST

A champion gro
of exhibition on
has spoken out a
neighbouring al
owner mistaken
bent over the to
his prize exhibit
fortnight too ear

Mr James Roy S
stated "although
daft buggers tho
were deeing us a
they've succeed
knackin me cha
this year. The sa
couple also lifte
main crop tatties
weeks too early
Amateurs!"

"Ah couldn't de
as a've had a he
problem"

Newspaper Boy

The Naughty Newspaper Boy

Grandma taught me to knit with bone needles and re cycled wool. When a ganzie was outgrown, we would unravel the wool to re use. I loved that, the wool had a kink when it was pulled out and Gran would pop it over my hands and roll it into a new ball ready for the next creation. It was like magic!

k.	knit
sts	stitches
rep	repeat
g.st	garter stitch (every row knit)
p	purl
tog	together
dec	decreasing

florrie

Repeat with the remaining pieces. Press seams open. Sew the 2 pieces RST along the straight sides leaving the waist and legs bottoms open. Fit to Norman tucking one side of the shirt under the waistline & leaving the other side hanging out. **See photo.** Stitch the shorts onto the waist. Gather the legs and secure in place.

Cut a 1" strip of felt and thread on a buckle. Place it around Norman's waist and sew in place.

To make the boots

Make a freezer paper template JJ on Page 63. Cut 4 from felt. Put 2 together and sew around as indicated on the pattern, repeat with remaining pieces. Fit boots to Norman, sew in place.

To make the waistcoat

Make freezer paper templates KK & LL on Page 63. Using felt, sew each front piece to the back RST, turn through and add buttons to one side. Take a 2" square of felt and stitch to the front of the waist coat on 3 sides to form a pocket. Fit to Norman.

To make Norman's bag

From felt cut 2 x 7" squares and 1" x 20". Place the 2 squares together & sew three sides, add the strip to each edge to form a handle.

Add rolled papers to the bag. If you want to make a catapult like Norman find a small 'Y' shaped twig and add a rubber band. **See photo.**

To make Norman's Cap

With no 10 (3.0mm, US 3) needles, cast on 66 sts. and work 1 inch. k.1, p.1 rib.

Continue in g.st until cap measures 2".

Now comes the shape bit –

1st row * k.2 tog, k.9; rep. from * to end

2nd and alternate rows, P.

3rd row *k.2 tog, k.8; rep. from * to end.

Continue in this way working 1 st. less between the the decs. Until 18 sts remain.

Break the wool and thread through the remaining sts, draw up tightly and fasten off.

Make a brim by turning up a section of the rib and whip stitch it into place.

Norman's Scarf

With no 10 (3.0mm, US 3) needles cast on 10 stitches and knit in g.st until the scarf measures 22" Cast off.

We have chosen tweed effect wool to use, don't worry too much about the ply, the cap will just be slightly larger or smaller depending on which wool you use.

DISTURBANCE ON PAPER ROUND

Sgt Biff had to intervene and stop Mrs Cannybody from strangling her newspaper boy Norman. She explained that Norman crumpled her newspaper up when pushing it through the letter box. This made is difficult to cut up and use in the netty!

Her man had nowt to go on.

Both parties have been shown the error of their ways by Sgt Biff.

There were no arrests.

FLORRIE BETTY'S DAY OU

Local authors Miss and Miss Betty org a trip to Holy Islan Saturday for 10 loc children and their p The Charrabang pi them up from outs Co-operative Store for the trip. Time w the essence becaus crossing is only pas twice a day to the i

Misses F & B prov refreshments on ar at their small cottag then the fun started adults had the oppo to sample the local however Mr Treml a little too much an to be carried back t cottage. Pheobe We was sick after three willicks but genera children had great t eve a Pu o

Canny Keepsake Box

Eee, when I think back

When we lived in Long Row, Mam gave me a box to keep my treasures in, I think it was an old cigar box; she used to keep candle bits in. Eee, when I think back, you could hardly call them treasures! I had some pretty buttons my sister cut off her best dress, an old brooch of a dragonfly me mam gave me with a broken clasp and an old thimble. I probably had more but I cannot mind on. I tried to make a cover for it but it was never a great success, still I have fond memories of that box.

florrie

34

Boxes crop up everywhere in Beamish Museum, from the beautiful hat boxes in the haberdashery department to the utility boxes at the railway station. We have designed a simple box to use as you wish. Our box opens flat so could be used to store our sewing.

What you need

Fabric A,B,C & D
20cms (8")

Bosal Craft-tex 20cms (8")

Grosgrain ribbon
1.1m (40")

Lace: 1m (30")

Finished Size: 7" x 7" x 7" approx

Cutting

Fabric A & B
cut 1 x 6½" x 19" & 2 x 6½" squares

Fabric C & D
cut 1 x 7" square & 4 x 7" x 2½"

Bosal Craft-tex
cut 5 x 5½" squares,
1 x 6" square & 4 x 6" x 1½"

How to make it

To make the box, take the long pieces of fabrics A & B, with RST sew around leaving one short side open. Turn through & press. Insert a 5½" square of Bosal ensuring it butts up to the sewn short edge. Sew across the fabric, at the edge of the Bosal. (This make a side of the box). Repeat with another square of Bosal. Insert a 3rd square of Bosal and turn under the open edges so that it is in line with the last edge of the Bosal. Stitch opening closed.

To make the remaining side pieces take a Fabric A & B 6½" square. Place RST & sew around 3 sides. Turn through & press. Insert a 5½" square of Bosal. Turn under the edges & sew along the edge. Repeat with the remaining two 6½" Fabrics A & B.

Refer to the photo for placement and sew the two squares to the main piece using a zig zag stitch on your machine.

Cut ribbon into 4 equal pieces and referring to photo for placement sew in place.

Bring the corners together with the ribbon and make a nice bow.

To make the lid using the C & D fabrics, repeat the instructions for the box base. You will have one square and 4 side pieces completed.

Refer to the photo for placement and sew the four sides to the square using a zig zag stitch. Pull the corners together and whip stitch in place, to form the lid.

Cover the stitching with lace. **See photo.**

'Mam's Memory Book' fits perfectly in the box.

Mam's Memory Book

Ledgers and beautifully bound books are on display in the Offices, Bank, and Stationers at Beamish Museum.

Mam's Memory Book looks like four book spines on a shelf or can be displayed in a Carousel fashion. Mam has added treasured letters and photographs to hers; she has another one which she pins her jewellery onto. The book fits perfectly into the Canny Keepsake Box on page 34.

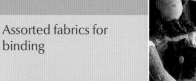

What you need

8 x 12" squares of assorted fabrics	Assorted fabrics for binding
H460: 30cms (12")	

Finished Size: 11" x 5½" approx

Cutting

H640 cut 4 x 12" squares

Cut assorted fabrics for binding

How to make it

Layer up a square of H640 between 2 squares of fabric and quilt as desired. Repeat with the remaining squares. Cut all the squares to 11" and bind using your preferred method or see Work Basket.

Fold each square in half and sew down the middle. **See photo.** Fold along the sewn edge, this makes a spine. Place 2 folded pieces together lining up the spines. Secure one front and one back with a stitch in each corner. **See photo.** Repeat this process adding the other two folded pieces. **See photo.**

To make the pockets on each page fold them 'page' in half on the diagonal. The first page fold out and second page folds under, **see photo.** Repeat for all pages. Embellish as desired.

The book will stand in a carousel fashion, lay flat or sit on a shelf (to look like 4 books).

Florrie keeps her special photos & letters in her Memory Book.

This book fits perfectly in the Canny Keepsake Box.

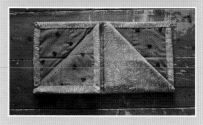

FLOWER FRILLS

If you want to make the flower on the Mam's Memory Book you will need a piece of fabric 36" x 2". Fold in half lengthwise and sew down the long edge. Turn through, and make a gather along the long edge. Pull and gather and form a flower, stitch in place as you go. Hide the centre with a nice button.

Catch up at Chapel

Postcards were really important to us in them days. It wasn't on to be fifteen and have a lad so we had to tell a fib or two, but we didn't do owt wrong like that. We would send each other postcards to arrange to meet, you could send it in the morning and he would get it in the afternoon! We would write in code and use other names. 'Jane Anne Teacake' was a popular name to stay anonymous. Chapel was our excuse to meet; we would meet in the chapel arch and do our courting.

Florrie

Picture Postcards

The postcard was the e-mail or text of the period. It was possible to post a card in the morning and have it delivered in the afternoon. They were often used to make arrangements and keep in touch. Some of the examples we have seen are for secret courting. Marvellous.

What you need

Background fabric 20cms x 14cms (8" x 5½")	Weaveline 20cms x 14cms (8" x 5½")
Stranded cotton	Buttons & Ribbons
Fabric glue	Easel card (Optional)

Finished Size: 6" x 4" approx

How to make it

Trace the stitchery pattern of your choice from Pages 58 & 59 onto the centre of the fabric. Place the weaveline onto the back. All stitching is completed with 2 strands of embroidery thread. Embellish as desired.

Betty has covered the picture board of an easel card using fabric glue, wrapping the edges over. She has displayed them this way adding ribbons. They would also make a lovely wall hanging, a greetings card or why not incorporate them into another project for example the bib of the apron on Page 50.

Is it better to have loved and lost?

Here are a couple of the messages Florrie found on the back of her old postcards, circa 1919

Dear James

Meet me at the Railway Bridge tonight at 7pm. If I'm there before you, I will put a stone on the wall; if you are there before me knock it off.

**I am yours
Etc**

James

Just a few lines to tell you I have jilted you. You cannot be the man you should be, I cannot marry you, so we will break off the engagement. Your ring will follow shortly.

Jane Ann Teacake

Transport Cushion

Always wanted a bike

I was in me teens and I wanted a bike but we couldn't afford it and I kept yammering on like a bairn. Me mother says 'I've got a little bit of money in the store' in them days they had dividends, it you bought a certain amount of stuff you got it put in the book and it mounted up, here it had mounted after a canny few years but she wasn't supposed to have that, she says 'if I divn't spend it they'll just take if off us' that's how I got the bike.

florrie

The Garage in the town centre is packed with vintage items relating to transport. Trams, trains, cars and buses are just some of the vehicles on show at Beamish Museum and we have used a couple of these as inspiration for our cushion.

What you need

Fabric for front Fat Quarter	Calico Fat Quarter
Fabric for back 75cms (29")	Assorted fabrics for appliqué
Wadding Fat Quarter	Binding 20cms (8")

Finished Size: 22" x 14" approx

Cutting

Background cut 1 x 24" x 16"

Wadding cut 1 x 24" x 16"

Calico cut 1 x 24" x 16"

Backing cut 2 x 14½" x 28½"

Binding cut 3 x 2½" strips

How to make it

Using the templates on Page 60 & 62 applique the pieces onto the background fabric using your preferred method. **See photo for placement.**

Layer the front of the cushion onto the wadding and calico and quilt as desired.

Trim down to 22½" x 14½".

Fold the backing fabrics in half WST and press. Place on to the reverse of the appliquéd front. Overlap the backing fabrics so that they create an envelope backing. The raw edges are to match.

Bind the edges using your preferred method or see Work Basket.

Afternoon Refreshments

More tea Vicar?

Miss Honey Bun owns the
little tea shop
It's where all the ladies
like to stop
For a slice of cake and
a pot of tea
When they are out on the town
On a spending spree

Hare of the Dog

The Sun Inn is the public house in the town centre at Beamish Museum. With roaring fires most of the year, it has a warm and welcoming atmosphere. The walls are decorated with pieces of taxidermy which were fashionable in the period. Such trophies are now made from wood and metal for interior design, our Hare is a fabric re-creation, stylish with a hint of the past.

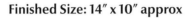

What you need

Fabric A sides of head & ears 20cms (8")	Fabric C to cover canvas Fat Quarter
Fabric B face & ears 20cms (8")	Crafters cord or linen thread
Canvas 12" x 10"	Timtex 10cms
Scraps of felt	Glue gel/fabric glue
Buttons & ribbon	Staple gun
Toy filling	Freezer paper

Finished Size: 14" x 10" approx

How to make it

Make freezer paper templates of all the pieces required for this project.

To make the head

Use template S on page 54 and cut 2 pieces from Fabric A.

From Fabric B cut a 2½" strip the full WOF. Pin this strip to one of the template S pieces, RST and sew in place leaving the neck open as indicated on the template. Repeat for the other side. Turn through. Trim the excess fabric. Stuff firmly and sew opening closed.

To make the ears

Use template T on page 55 and cut 2 pieces from Fabrics A & B, and 2 of the Timtex. Place Fabrics A & B RST and sew together leaving the bottom open, turn through, insert the Timtex and sew the opening closed. Sew a line down the centre of the ears. **See photo.**

Attach the ears to the head, refer to the photo for placement & secure with buttons.

Using the templates for the eyes, nose & mouth on page 59 add features using felt. We added buttons to the eyes. **See photo.**

Thread lengths of crafters cord through the sides of the face, to make the whiskers.

See photo. You could use linen thread as an alternative.

To cover the canvas

Put a thin covering of fabric glue onto the front of the canvas board and then carefully cover it with the fabric. Let the glue dry before stretching it around the side of the canvas and securing with staples.

Position the head onto the canvas and secure by sewing with linen thread or using a strong glue. We used a combination of the two. A curved or a long dolls needle would make this job easier. Allow the glue to dry over night.

To make the bow tie

Make a bow tie from wide ribbon, add buttons and glue in place at the neck. **See photo.**

Florrie & Betty would like to make it known that no animals were harmed during the making of this project.

Wine Gums and Sherry

Florrie's high on wine gums
Betty is sipping sherry
They are having a very
*   happy day*
They certainly are quite merry
Now they are trying some beer
I think it's a bit mistake
Tomorrow morning
*   they will have*
A truly huge headache!

Tea Cup & Saucer

Bring back the days when everyone had a best tea or coffee service. There are wonderful examples of china and everyday wares in the Co-operative store. There are also great examples of needlework items in the haberdashery department. Our saucer is half scissor keep and half needle keep. Floral patterns mimic the patterns on the china and there is even enough room for a couple of biscuits.

What you need

Tea Cup Pin Cushion

Bosal Craft-tex
8cms x 20cms (3" x 8")

Fabric A outside cup
10cms (4")

Fabric B pin cushion
Fat 16th

Toy filling

Button

Saucer Scissor & Needle Keep

Large circles Fat Quarter or 4 x 16ths of different fabrics

Centre circles Fat 16th

Wadding Fat 16th

Lace 60cms (24")

Heat 'n' Bond Ultra

Tea Cup Pin Cushion

Finished Size: 3" x 4" approx

Cutting

Bosal Craft-tex cut 1 x 3" x 8" and 1 x ½" x 6½"

Fabric A cut 1 x 4" x 18" & 1½" x 15"

Fabric B cut 1 circle template F Page 55

How to make it

From Fabric A take the larger piece of fabric fold in half lengthwise RST and sew down the long sides. Turn through and insert the Bosal Craft-tex between the fabrics. Fold in the raw edges to neaten and sew the opening closed. Carefully bend into a circle and sew sides together. **See photo.**

Make the handle in the same way as the cup. Fold handle in half lengthwise, sew together and attach to the cup covering the join. Stitch in place at the top and bottom of the cup, add a button to the bottom of the handle.

Take the circle of Fabric B turn in the edges a ¼" and using a running stitch sew around the edge. Place a small amount of toy filling in the centre, gather up, adding more toy filling. Secure. Insert into the Cup.

Saucer Scissor & Needle Keep

Finished Size: 8" x 8" approx

Cutting

Make 4 circles of template F Page 55. You can use as many fabrics as you wish

Cut one wadding of template F page 55

Cut 3 circles of template G Page 55 from Heat 'n' Bond Ultra

How to make it

Take 2 of the large circles, place RST and sew around the outer edge. Make a slit in the centre of one of the circles, turn through and press. Repeat with the remaining 2 large circles but place wadding on the back of one of these before sewing.

Fuse the small circles of Heat 'n' Bond Ultra to the remaining fabric, and cover the openings on the large circles with 2 of the small circles.

Layer the 2 completed circles, with the fused circles in the middle, and sew across the centre of them. From the centre sew 2 lines to make the segments, **see photo.**

Fuse the remaining circle to the centre of the top of the saucer, embellish with lace.

Good Mix

Papa is a well known dentist

Mama is a leading light

In the Ladies Quilting Society

They meet every

*   Wednesday night*

Our parlour maid is Daisy

Our cook is Mrs Brown

She is known to make

*   the best cake*

Of any one in town

Floral Placemats

The Tea Rooms allow the visitor to Beamish Museum to have a welcome break for refreshments. Afternoon tea is very popular again; Florrie and Betty had a tea party for the recent Royal Wedding. We have designed these placemats which are inspired by the many floral wallpapers and specifically the flower on the Co-operative building.

What you need to make 2 placemats

Background fabric Fat Quarter	Flower centre scrap of fabric
Flower fabric Fat Quarter	Backing Fat Quarter
Cutlery holder fabric Fat Quarter	Binding 20cms (8″)
H630 Fat Quarter	Knives, forks & spoons
Wadding Fat Quarter	One lovely dining room table

Finished Size: 16½″ x 12½″ approx

Cutting for one Placemat

Background cut 1 x 18″ x 14″

Binding cut 2 x 2½″ strips

How to make it

Make a freezer paper template J of the cutlery holder on Page 55.

Place cutlery holder fabrics RST, adding the H630 on one side. Using the freezer paper template as a sewing guide, sew around the shape. To turn through make a small cut in the lower part of one of the fabrics, and press. To cover the opening fuse a small piece of fabric in place.

Position the cutlery holder to the right of the background fabric, pin and sew in place. **See photo.**

Trace 5 petals template K and a flower centre template H onto Heat 'n' Bond Lite on Page 55.

See photo for placement and fuse petals and the flower centre to the background fabric. Blanket stitch around the each piece.

Layer onto the wadding and backing fabric.

Quilt as desired.

Trim to 16½″ x 12½″ and bind using your preferred method or see Work Basket.

Our own Shop

Me sister in law asked if we would fancy her shop. She went back to her house and we went into the shop. I had it for three years and my name was on the top outside. I ran the shop all day everyday, except for a Wednesday afternoon when I went to the wholesalers in Newcastle. It was just sweets and cakes at first, but I come to have a drapery and other bits and pieces after a while.

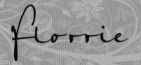

Coconut Cannies

You will need

2½ oz (70gms) self raising flour

1½ oz (40gms) caster sugar

2oz (60gms) margarine

A couple drops of vanilla essence

Desiccated coconut

Glace cherries

Cream the margarine, sugar and essence in a bowl

Add flour and mix thoroughly

Roll into approx 20 balls and roll them liberally in the coconut

Pop onto a greased baking tray and flatten slightly (don't be too heavy handed!)

Add a cherry aesthetically in the middle of each Coconut Canny

Bake in moderate oven for 15 to 20 minutes

Mmmmmmmmm (you don't have to share these)

Betty's Best Pinny

The photographs in the archives at Beamish Museum show aprons very much in the style of our Pinny. The aprons in the public sphere were quite elaborate with frills and always starched, those in private domestic homes were less formal. The buttons on our apron allow adjustability so that one size can fit all.

What you need

Main fabric 1m (1 yard)	**Fabric for squares**
Pocket fabric Fat 16th	Fabric A 10cms (4")
Fabric for straps 30cms (12")	Fabric B 10cms (4")
Duck Cloth 1m (1 yard)	Fabric C 25cms (9")
2 buttons	Binding 50cms (18")

Finished Size: 38" x 35" approx

Cutting

Main fabric cut 2 x 7½" squares, cut in half on the diagonal to make 4 triangles, cut 1 x 21½" x 35½"

Duck Cloth cut 1x 10½" square, 1 x 21½" x 35½", 1x 10½" x 7½"

Straps cut 4 x 3" strips

Binding cut 5 x 2½" strips.

Pocket cut 1 x 10½" x 7½"

How to make it

You will need to make 6 square in a square blocks as per Florrie's Medallion Quilt on Pages 16-18.

To make the Bib

Take one square in a square block and add main fabric triangles to the sides, **see photo**. Sew the remaining triangles to opposite sides, and press. Trim the square to 10½".

Make the straps

Fold the fabric RST lengthwise and sew down the long edge, and one short edge. Turn through and press.

Repeat to make the other straps.

Place the bib block on top of the Duck Cloth 10½" square, WST. Position 2 of the straps on the block. Bind 3 sides using your preferred method or see Work Basket sewing the shoulder straps into the binding.

Main Part of Apron

Take the 5 remaining square in a square blocks and sew them in a row; this is the bottom edge of the apron. Sew this strip to the larger piece of main fabric and press.

Now place the main part of the apron on top of the Duck Cloth. WST

Measure 2 inches down each side of the main part of the apron and position a strap to each side. Baste in place.

Centre the Bib onto the top of the main piece RST sew using a scant ¼" seam allowance.

Bind all edges of the main part of the apron as before making sure that you incorporate the bib and the side straps.

To make Pocket

Place the pocket fabric and Duck Cloth RST. Sew around all sides leaving a small gap for turning. Turn through and press.

Position the pocket onto the main part of the apron and top stitch 3 sides, **see photo.**

Sew a button to each side of the apron just above the side straps.

Make a button hole in each of the shoulder straps. The position of the button hole is up to you or if you are making the apron as a gift make several button holes on each strap so that it can be adjusted.

The shoulder straps cross over at the back making the apron very comfortable to wear.

Florrie & Betty's Work Basket

All kinds of
lovely things
are hidden
away in
Florrie &
Betty's Work
Basket,
it is always
a treat to
explore

*Mam used to drive me dad
crazy when she was sewing.
She wasn't a tidy worker,
I think she did it deliberately*

florrie

CONFUSION ARISES OVER STITCHES

A local member of The Women's Institute would like put the record straight and has said, "She knows her french knots from her back stitches and can point out a running stitch at 20 yards".

Allegations of a scant disregard were raised when it was found that incorrect stitches were used on a current 'stitchery pattern'. It was also alleged that there was also stitching taking place under the influence of sherry.

A statement was later released from The Women's Institute stating sherry is used for medicinal purposes only.

FRENCH KNOT DIAGRAM

BACK STITCH DIAGRAM

RUNNING STITCH DIAGRAM

Templates

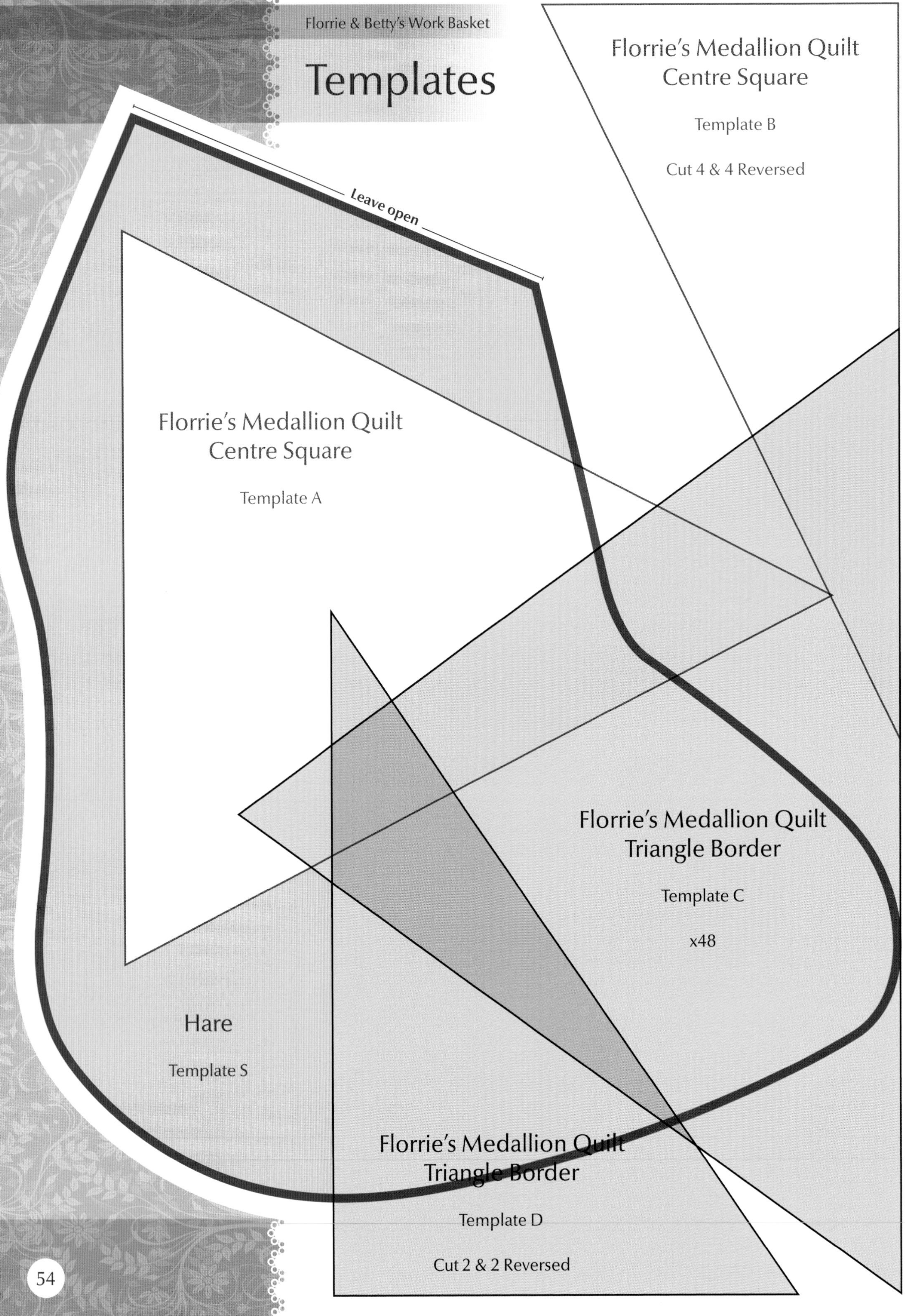

Florrie's Medallion Quilt
Centre Square

Template B

Cut 4 & 4 Reversed

Leave open

Florrie's Medallion Quilt
Centre Square

Template A

Florrie's Medallion Quilt
Triangle Border

Template C

x48

Hare

Template S

Florrie's Medallion Quilt
Triangle Border

Template D

Cut 2 & 2 Reversed

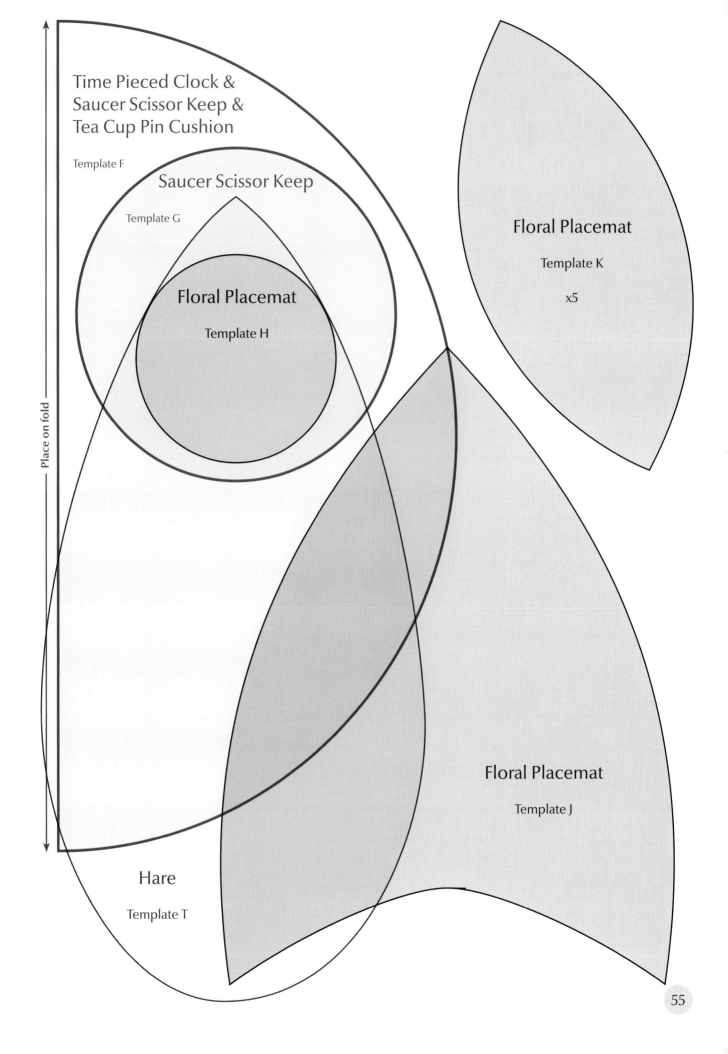

Time Pieced Clock &
Saucer Scissor Keep &
Tea Cup Pin Cushion

Template F

Place on fold

Saucer Scissor Keep

Template G

Floral Placemat

Template H

Floral Placemat

Template K

x5

Floral Placemat

Template J

Hare

Template T

55

Templates

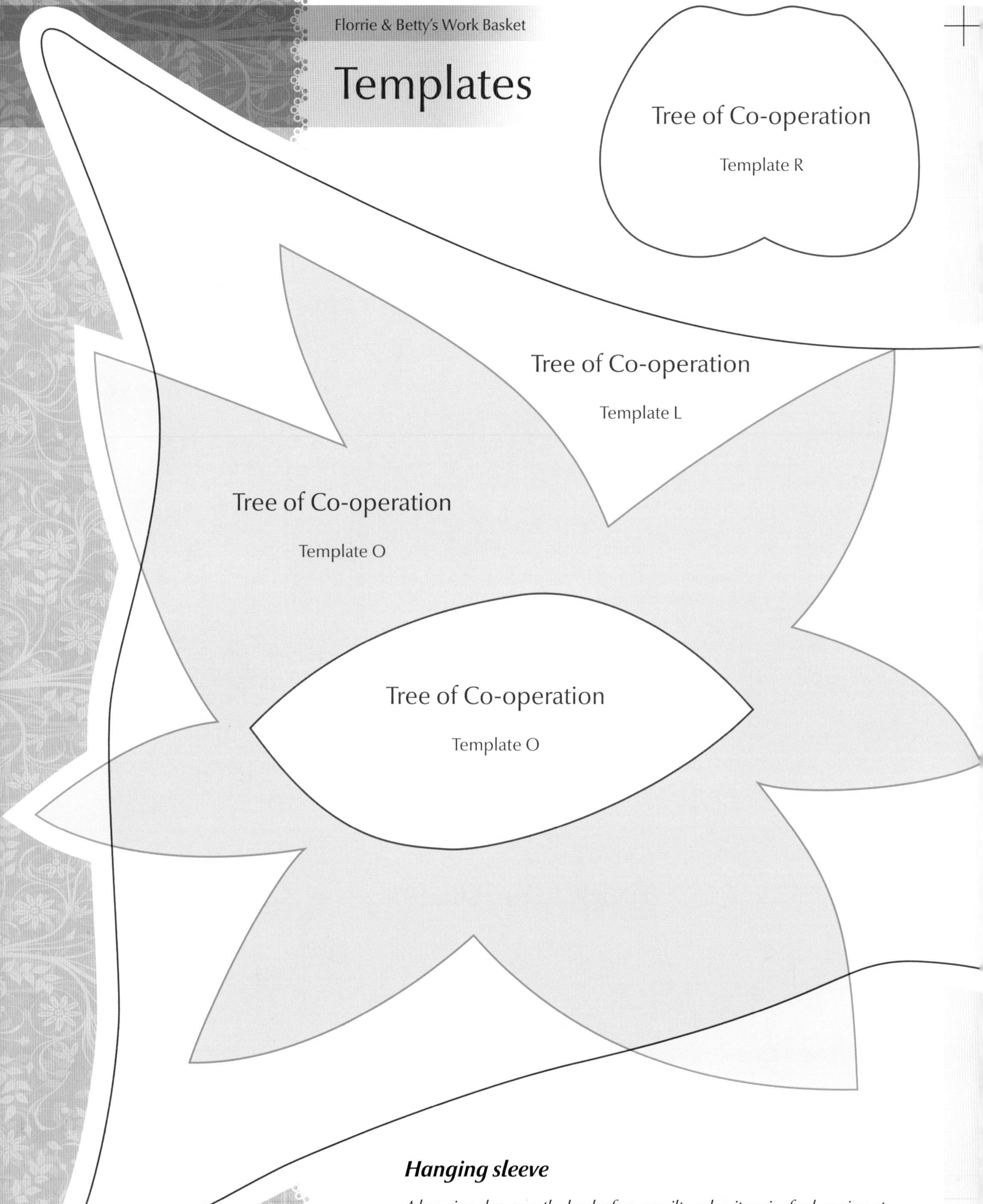

Tree of Co-operation

Template R

Tree of Co-operation

Template L

Tree of Co-operation

Template O

Tree of Co-operation

Template O

Hanging sleeve

A hanging sleeve on the back of your quilt makes it easier for hanging at home or in a quilt show.

Cut fabric 8″ wide and the width of your quilt.

Hem the short edges. Place RST and sew the long edge. Turn though and press the seam to the middle. Centre onto the top of the reverse of the quilt approx. ½″ from the binding and whipstitch in place.

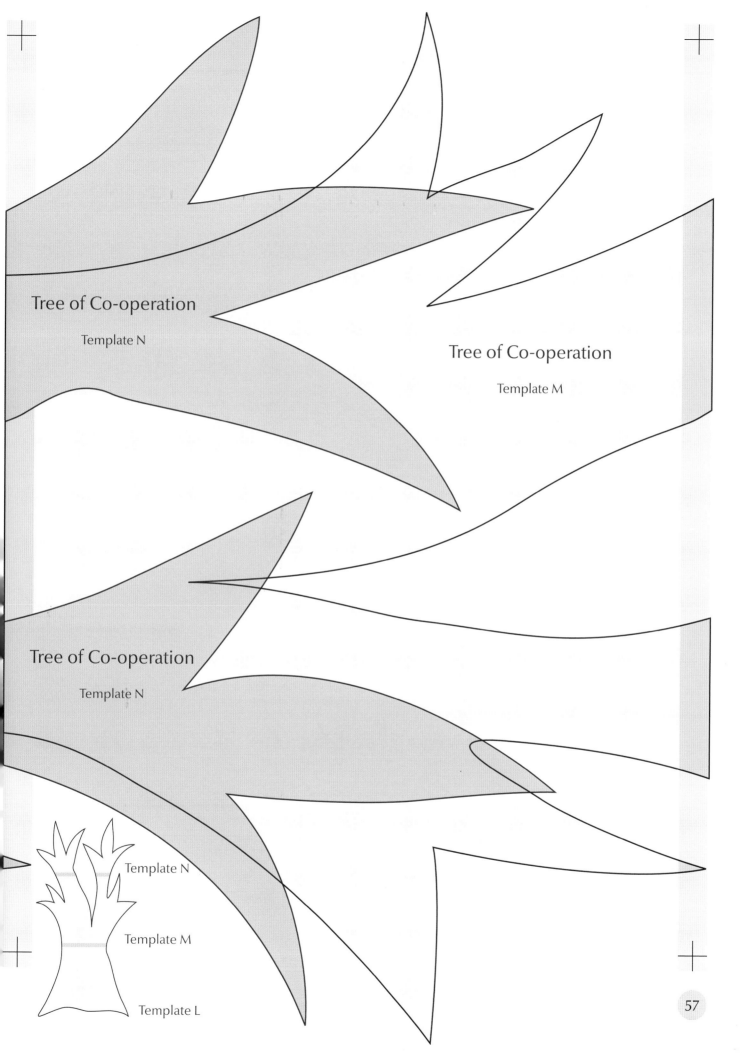

Tree of Co-operation

Template N

Tree of Co-operation

Template M

Tree of Co-operation

Template N

Template N

Template M

Template L

Templates

Layering up a Quilt

The quilt sandwich is made up of 3 layers, the quilt top, wadding & backing fabric. Ensure the wadding and backing fabric is approximately 3" larger on each side than the quilt top.

Lay the fabric on a flat surface and lay the wadding on top. Smooth out any wrinkles. Lay the quilt top in the centre. Baste the 3 layers in a grid. You are now ready to start quilting.

Quilting

Quilting stitches hold all three layers together and can create texture.

You can hand or machine quilt. If using a sewing machine increase the stitch length. Some machines have a setting which will automatically do this.

If sewing by hand use a quilting needle or between and do a running stitch through all 3 layers. Do not worry about doing small stitches it is better that all your stitches are the same length. The more you do the better you will get. Betty prefers to use a Quilt hoop available from your local quilting shop.

Binding Tips

Cut 2½" strips, press WST. Sew onto the right side of quilt, matching raw edges. Turn over and whip stitch in place.

Paper Bag bottom

This makes the base stand flat. It can be used during bag making or in our case when we made the doll.

Pull the back and the front apart. Align the side seams with the bottom seam and also align the edges of the squares. Stitch seam across the square, repeat on the other side.

Fusible Appliqué

Our preferred fusible paper is Heat 'n' Bond. The Lite needs to be sewn in place the Ultra does not.

Trace the design onto the smooth side of fusible paper. Cut out roughly (so you can still see your drawn line).

Fuse to the reverse of the fabric, using a hot iron, no steam. Do not overheat as it reverses the process.

Cut out the design on the line, and peel off the backing paper. Position onto the background fabric and fuse in place with the iron as before.

florrie and bettys...

NEW

Chocolates

So Canny

Pity we don't Share

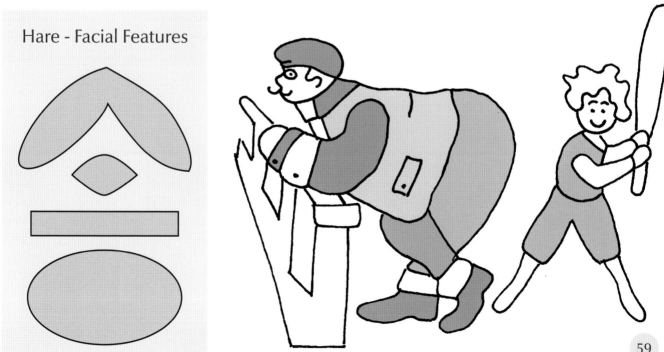

Hare - Facial Features

Templates

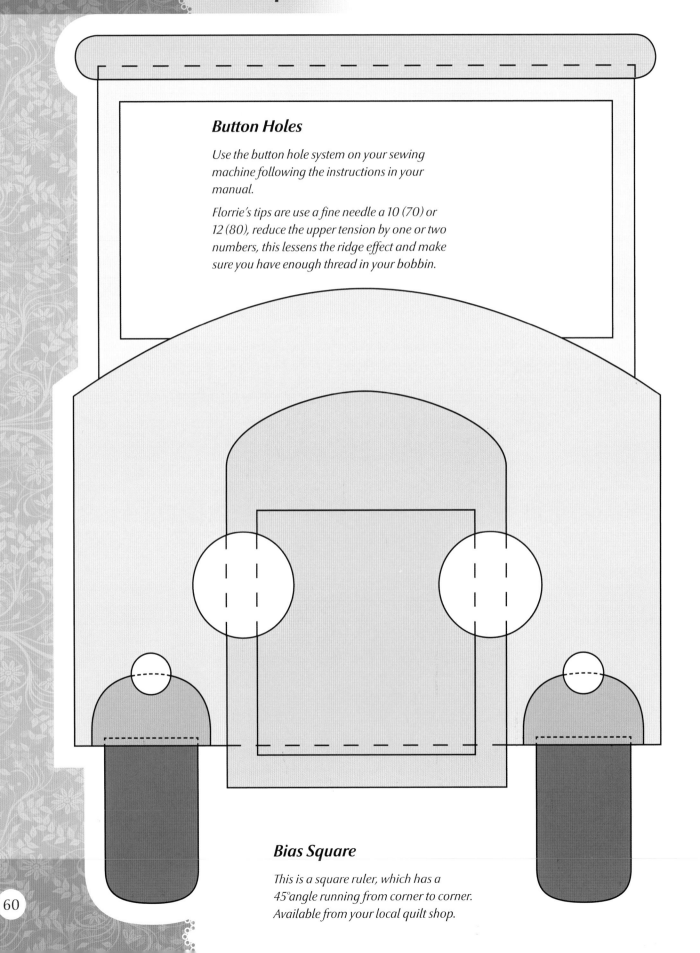

Button Holes

Use the button hole system on your sewing machine following the instructions in your manual.

Florrie's tips are use a fine needle a 10 (70) or 12 (80), reduce the upper tension by one or two numbers, this lessens the ridge effect and make sure you have enough thread in your bobbin.

Bias Square

This is a square ruler, which has a 45°angle running from corner to corner. Available from your local quilt shop.

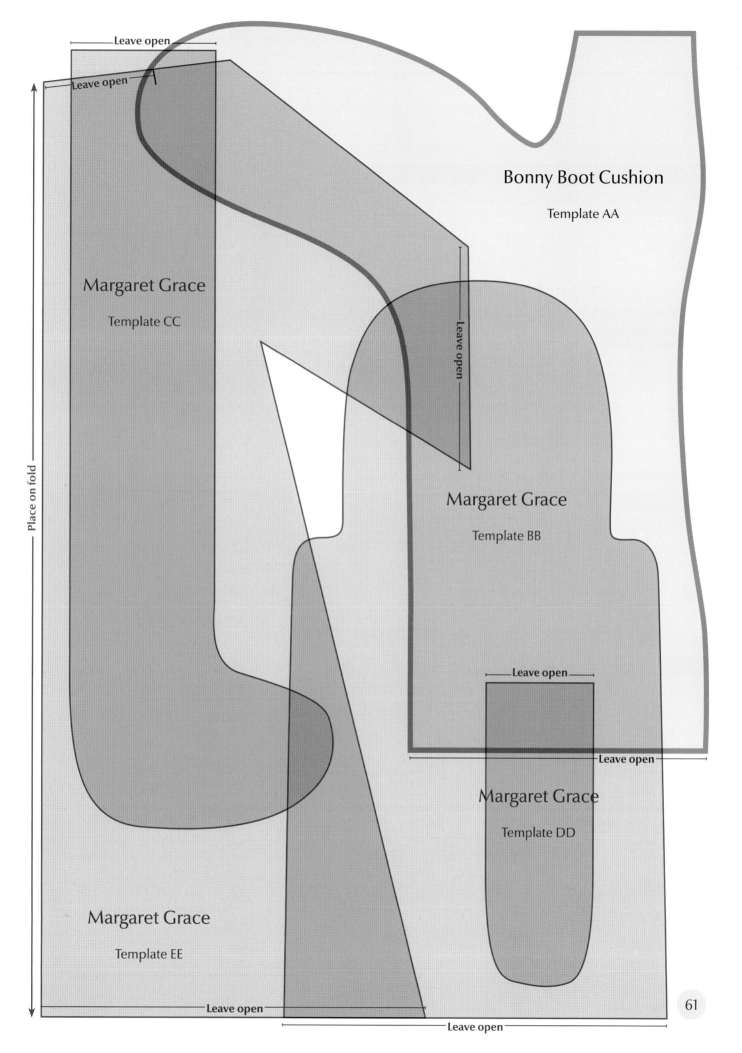

Leave open

Leave open

Bonny Boot Cushion

Template AA

Margaret Grace

Template CC

Place on fold

Leave open

Margaret Grace

Template BB

Leave open

Margaret Grace

Template DD

Leave open

Margaret Grace

Template EE

Leave open

Leave open

61

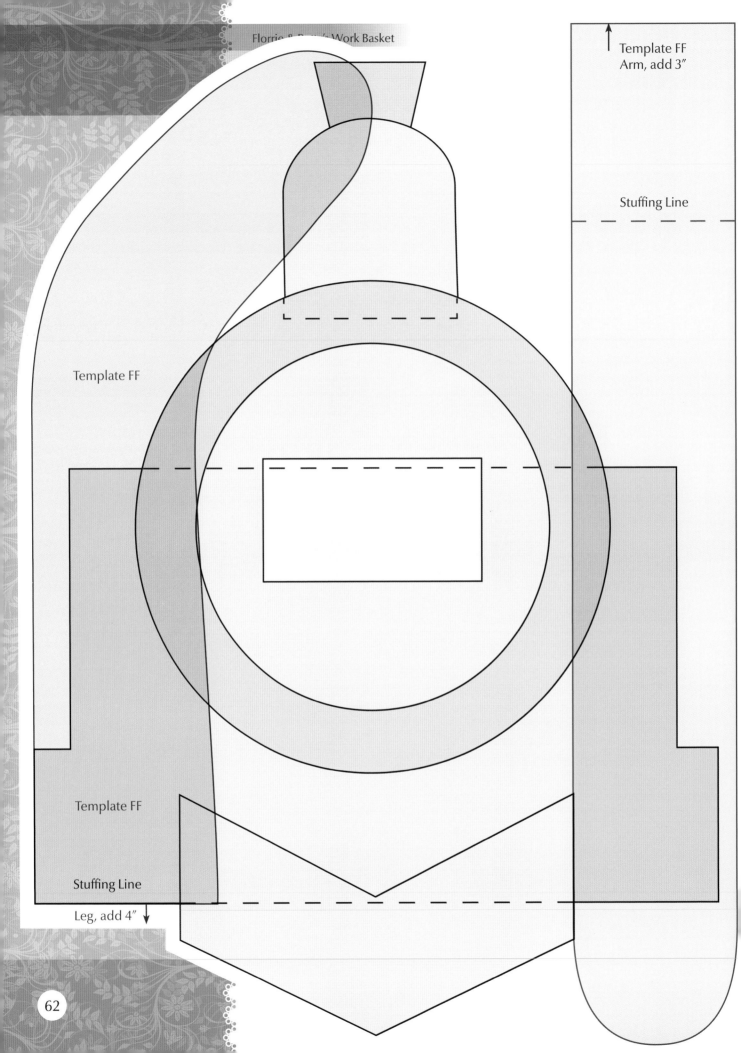

Template FF
Arm, add 3"

Stuffing Line

Template FF

Template FF

Stuffing Line

Leg, add 4"

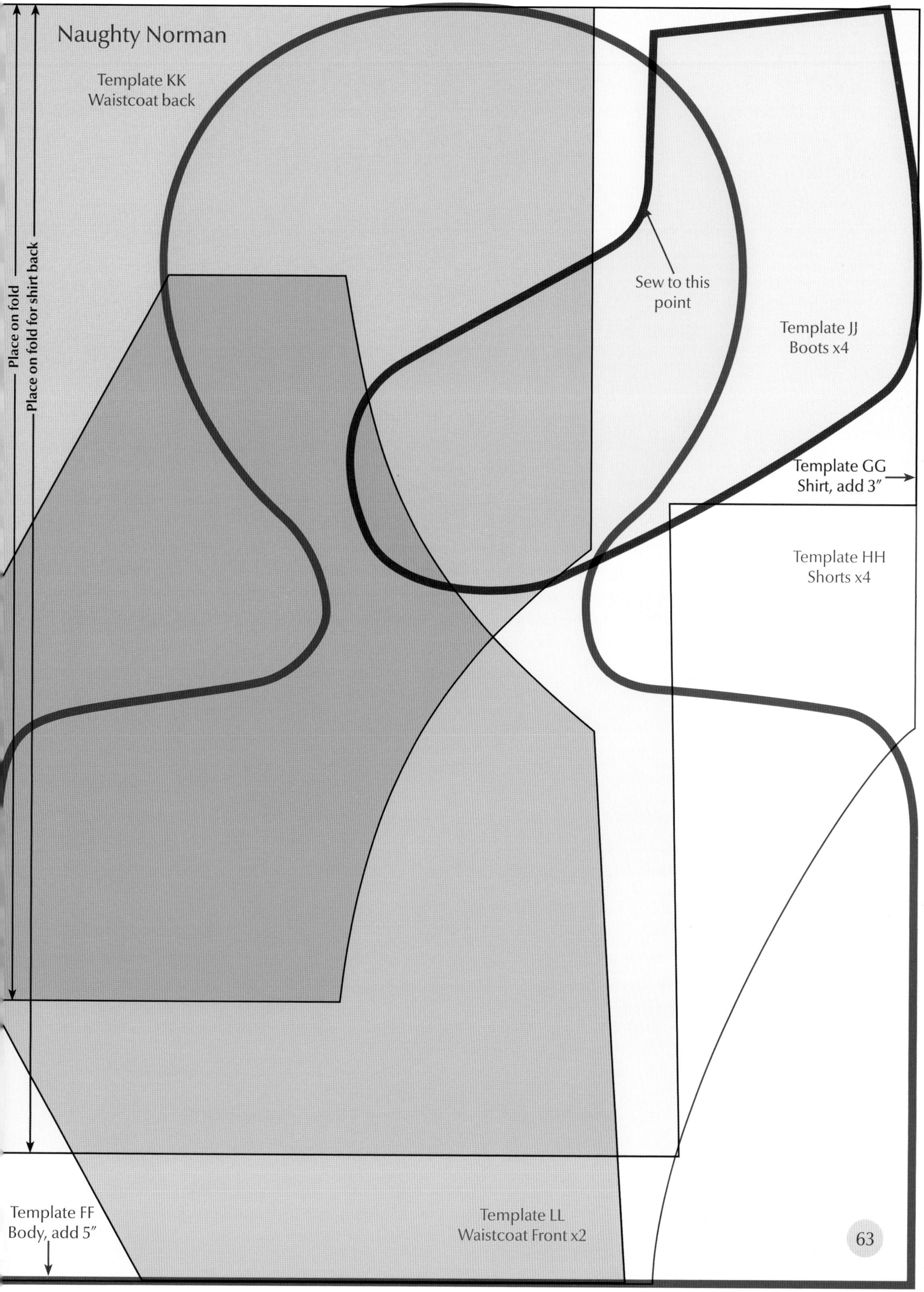

Naughty Norman

Template KK
Waistcoat back

Place on fold

Place on fold for shirt back

Sew to this
point

Template JJ
Boots x4

Template GG
Shirt, add 3"

Template HH
Shorts x4

Template FF
Body, add 5"

Template LL
Waistcoat Front x2

About the materials used...

Time of our lives

From a Colliery Village to an Edwardian Town, we are having the time of our lives!
We are so lucky to have good people around us and long may it continue.
Let's raise a glass to continued smiles and laughter.

Windham Fabrics have been used for all the projects in Shopping Days. They are ideal for the Edwardian period but we think you'll agree they work equally well today within a twenty first century setting.

The projects would lend themselves to contemporary and vintage fabric ranges, the Hare of the Dog looks lovely in primary colours for a child's room and the quilt is beautiful in any colour you choose.

Thank you to Windham Fabrics for endorsing Shopping Days and for their continued support and encouragement. A big thank you to Laura who never fails to help however she can.

In addition to vintage laces and buttons we have used Coats UK threads throughout.

Marvellous!

Florrie
& Betty

"Shopping Days"
is lovingly
dedicated to
Betty Garland
and
Florrie Oxtoby

We Raise our Glasses to....

Beamish Museum

For another fantastic setting. In particular Jacki for her enthusiasm and help. She's one of the family now!

The Delaval Arms, Old Hartley

An additional photographic location, with lovely views of St Mary's Lighthouse.

A huge 'Hipp Hipp Hooray' to...

Lady Margaret

Jackie O'Halloran

Sgt Biff

That right canny designer blokey

Terry Pinnegar Photography (page 40)

Florrie & Betty would like to remind you that they have a range of Greetings Cards, get in touch at sales@cannykeepsakes.co.uk